Molten Muse

Molten Muse

Kenneth Johnson

Clare Songbirds
Publishing House

Clare Songbirds Publishing House Poetry Series
ISBN 978-1-957221-14-4
Clare Songbirds Publishing House
Molten Muse © 2024 Kenneth Johnson

Printed in the United States of America
FIRST EDITION

140 Cottage Street
Auburn, New York 13021
www.claresongbirdspub.com

. . . and then, I have nature and art and poetry,
and if that is not enough, what is enough?
~Vincent van Gogh

Acknowledgments

Thank you to the editors of the following publications
in which these poems have previously appeared:

Beir Bua Journal: Rocket Launch
The Diaspora/UC Berkeley: The Brickworks
Elsewhere: Silk Dreams
Hitchlit Review: Manzanita
Humana Obscura: The Bristlecone Pine
Last Stanza Poetry Journal: The Bowline, The rain made it seem
San Antonio Review: As she was, Warehouse of Broken Wheels
Scavengers Literary Magazine: Bit Parts, Dream Thieves
Spillway 29 Journal: Blue Light, Kodokushi
Subterranean Blue Poetry: Shadow crafter
Talking River Review: Immaculate Deception, Molten Muse
Moon Rabbit, Tattooed Man

Mendocino lyrics in "She Rocked the Farfisa" by Doug Sahm, 1968

Contents

Along the Lake

She walked on a path
along the shore of the lake,

feeling the clam shells
beneath her bare feet.

A summer storm is coming
in off the gulf she thought

as she stood for a moment
taking in the summer sky

full of huge thunderclouds,
the breeze gaining strength,

a great egret slowly making
its way over the brackish water.

She smiled knowing the egrets
thrived now after near extinction.

She remembered her mother
wearing white plumed hats

and white gloves on Sundays,
those were different times.

The air was dense and warm
with the smell of oil and clay,

the sound of cars crossing
the causeway in the distance.

Tattooed Man

I am a tattooed man
like my Uncle Jerry

I sat on his lap as a child
smelling tobacco and green soap

while I traced the curves
of his life and imagined

the secrets that could be told
if the stars could speak

through the sweat and blood
and dank air and feral heat

given off by fluorescent tubes
with their buzzing ballasts

and phosphorus emitting light
like the North Star guiding us home

Manzanita

A bird sits alone on a branch
in the garden as we talk about
nature and lost souls. If there
is such a thing. The bird sings
to no one. Does it have a soul?
We could push everything aside
to reveal light breaking through
the trees. We could reveal secrets
if we knew what we believed.
Could we strip naked and reveal
our betrayals? There is a stream
that flows through this valley
in spring. The water gives shape
to our formless selves. It carries
us as we make our way across
the hills and through the skies.
It sustains us and the land as we
fashion myths from nothingness,
as we nurture carefully crafted
prophecies. We are surrounded
by small broadleaf trees bearing
fruit, not all of it edible. Manzanita
berries bloom in spring. The alluring
red fruit and flowers are edible.
They will sustain us if we fall.

As she was

breathing in the rain,
she felt the water
collect on her skin,
clinging to her
like a rose petal
holding on until
the very last moment

She closed her eyes
to remember a young girl
running, jumping,
stomping into a puddle
to watch her reflection
burst into pieces
to join the sky,
the river, the ocean,
ancient and foretelling

Moon Rabbit

There is a rabbit making tortillas on the surface of the moon. You can see it, if you look closely, as it stands over a comal heated using batteries from an abandoned go-kart. Lately, it has been thinking about installing solar because it's eco-friendly. It makes tacos on Saturdays to avoid being called a cliché. For special occasions, it makes tortillas pintadas with images of skulls or birds. It is said it saved a man on earth who later became a god. Now, Moon Rabbit can live on the moon rent free forever. On holidays, it makes tamales with salsa verde and tres leches cake for dessert.

BMX Moon Rabbit

Look closely at the moon on a clear night and you will see a rabbit cycling on the moon. It has a bike with big fat tires that leave tracks in billions of years old dust. It likes to ride BMX freestyle with no helmet, jumping over craters and space junk. Sometimes, it does tricks like the lookback or moto whip. It doesn't have to follow any rules because there are no sanctioning bodies or associations on the moon. During the day, after a night of riding, it makes mooncakes for lunch. When Year of the Rabbit rolls around, it gives them to all its friends. Its favorite is the lotus bean filling cake with a flakey crust.

Shadow crafter

blocking in scrubbing out
    defining eliminating
bring the sun in
       for a closer look
dots of light
    on the surface
sparkling embers
       floating on breaths
bits stuck in the tooth
    some in deep canyons
others barely visible
       some crevices deepened
some skimmed over
    shadows are formed
opaque objects block
    source light
       hard light
          soft light
       white light
    yellow light
nonblack shadows
    transparent layers
absorbed colors
       reflected colors
highlighting differentiating
        concealing revealing
organizing unifying
       weaving in and out
of visible degrees
       on an invisible scale

Warehouse of Broken Wheels

The grief counselor informed me
the free-trial subscription period

was ending soon, and it was time
to decide — enroll or cancel.

Eventually, it all comes 'round,
you said misery loves company,

yet the company closed up shop,
packed it in, left town, no notice,

not even a lousy fire sale,
not even for heaven's sake,

just flashes of light prints
dimming as they walk away.

Nothing to do now but take shelter
in a warehouse of broken wheels

Molten Muse

She posed for love
the search for truth
consumed by fire
in resplendent light
the exhilaration
of pouring her molten
self to cool and solidify
into the shape
of a hawk soaring high
on thermals while circling
unsuspecting prey
sometimes choosing to glide
low carefully observing
nuances of a surface
a patina burnished
into new lifeblood

Kodokushi

It hit me like a ton of something on a day I no longer remember. I think I read a ton of feathers weighs the same as a ton of bricks. An Italian guy dropped cannon balls from a tower. I don't remember why, something about gravity. I heard that from a tour guide, seems like a past life. It was the only time I ever left the country. There's still an old paper map on a table, with faded newspapers, photographs, and origami cranes. The din of cicadas is omnipresent as night now falls in pieces like rocks filling up this space, this overstuffed chair. There is a natural place for everything to seek. When the weight is overwhelming, I see myself imploding, spilling out onto the floor, only to be mopped up by a stranger.

Blue Light

I watched your body
fold into a crane
a thousand times

only to be converted
to ashes I set adrift
to float downstream

watching as you
swirled and slipped
around and through

leaves and twigs
nymphs and larvae
to where you finally

opened your mouth
swallowed the sea
became blue light

Immaculate Deception

Truth came in flashes,
evaporating each time
like rainwater on a dry lake
bed with wind stripping
the salt pan of vegetation
and expectations, making
it difficult to see clearly
through the mineral haze

Standing in the desert heat,
she remembered wanting
to believe in something,
to believe in anything,
trying to break the codes,
hoping to prevail one day
while sweeping up scattered
pieces of broken road signs

The air sticks in her throat,
temporarily paralyzing her
as she thinks about the books
she read about survival,
about the essential qualities
needed to live the best life,
how she had never taken time
to think about who wrote them

The rain made it seem

like we were on tv in a
black and white movie
characters on a storyboard
acting in a multilayered plot
umbrellas modifying remnants
of winter light reflections
archived memories stacked
on shelves of sleepless nights

I imagined the hole deeper
time slower words louder
than those spoken in shadows
of rolling posthumous clouds
indistinct syllables floating
like notes played on a distant
hill by a quartet of seasons
long since melded into one

desire pity love loss joy
mingling with damp steam
rising from the turned earth
reminds me of the times
we stayed awake all night
counting your wounds
measuring your scars
watching your mouth twitch
searching for the right words

Silk Dreams

He always wore silk clothing, no matter the occasion. In the garden, in the city, in the countryside. He drove a silk car and ate silk pancakes for breakfast. He walked a silk dog and married a silk woman, Iris, the woman of his silk dreams. He admired her satiny sheen that shimmered when the wind blew. He wove silk into every conversation he ever had. He spoke of ancient Asia and mulberry trees whenever possible, sericulture and insect larvae. One morning, he got up early to walk the dog before a light drizzle became rain. At breakfast with Iris, he felt the smooth silk tablecloth and said silk is one of the strongest natural fibers. Yes, she responded, but it loses about twenty percent of its strength when wet.

Dream Thieves

The palms looked like crepe paper flowers in the stifling heat, the chain-link fence like wings of a broken bird. What was left of a front lawn made the old wooden house look abandoned. She sat on the front porch while scanning the neighborhood for a glimpse of the intruders, thieves on wanted posters archived in her now impenetrable vault. She sat on her front porch every afternoon, sipping strong black coffee, hoping to spot the criminals who stole her dreams. She recalled the nights they broke into her home while she was sleeping. It didn't happen all at once. They chiseled away bit by bit, like master sculptors carefully following their preliminary sketches and well-crafted maquettes. One night, their work was complete, and they moved on. She figured they were most likely in one of those luxury town-homes in the mirrored high rises she could barely see on the distant hills overlooking the city. They were probably laughing, dining, watching big-ass televisions, and saying things like *my god, look at that view*. They had moved on, but they'd be back. She was sure of it.

The Brickworks

The first time I saw my daddy cry
was the day the tracks got pulled up.
The world had changed they said,
time had bypassed us they said.
The brickworks was forced to close,
it could no longer operate at a loss.

Loss is what tore apart my daddy
the day he cried. He could feel it
in his tired, brittle bones as he sat
staring out the window of our home
at the factory that was now nothing
more than an abstract pile of scrap iron.

A whirlwind of old torn newspapers
blew across the road, over the raised
gravel beds where the tracks once lay,
pushed against a sagging, rusted
chain-link fence. Yes sir, I can do that,
my daddy said under his breath,
yes sir, I can work weekends
and holidays, he was nodding his head,
yes sir, I can come in early, stay late.

The long mornings became the most
difficult part of the day. He and my
momma sat at our round wooden table,
doing their best to sip dark coffee and
eat buttered toast with homemade jam.
They were silent most mornings
before daddy went to the window to
monitor any changes. We used to play
outside that window, in the yard.
When he squinted, he could see us
laughing, running around through the
water whirling out of the sprinkler he
bought at now-closed A-1 Mercantile.
I remember my daddy's smile that day.

The Bristlecone Pine

A steadfast mother in ancient Mesopotamia
was teaching her daughter to weave wool
to provide warmth in the coming winter
of the river lands of the Fertile Crescent,
the life-sustaining Tigris and Euphrates,
as father directed water to desperate crops.

Somewhere just below the tree line in the
White Mountains of eastern California,
a seedling begins new life, its tentacle like
roots gripping into the rocky dolomite soil
as winds of fine sand cut through the dry
rain shadow of the Sierra Nevada Mountains.

Today, the antediluvian sentinel Methuselah
stands, the proud protector of the Great Basin
Bristlecone Pine progeny, its gnarled hardwood
arms reaching out like burghers cast in bronze,
nature's historic monument, a reminder to
remain open to mystery and wonder.

She Rocked the Farfisa

She rocked the Farfisa
in a dark cantina near the beach

Dancing on the stage all night
in throbbing multicolored lights

Mendocino, Mendocino,
Where life's such a groove

We cleared the walks with firecrackers,
lit up the waves with bottle rockets

We made love on sand under a pier,
made promises we knew we couldn't keep

Mendocino, Mendocino,
Where life's such a groove

Rocket Launch

Somewhere there's a map with photos
      of our faces
pressed against the glass of our windows,
staring out at geometric patterns generated
      by search algorithms.
Some concerned citizens filed a lawsuit,
their houses were bulldozed while they
      were buying groceries.
If I could build a rocket, I'd launch it into space.
I'd sell advertising and put company logos on all
      its visible parts.
As a kid, I pushed a corked bottle with a note
inside into the ocean while on a family vacation.
      I've never seen it again.

The Bowline

A thousand puzzle pieces lay scattered
    on the table,
dulled by multilayers of dust.
     It didn't start
that way, I had always intended
       to assess the damage
            dress the wounds
                salvage the remnants.

Following a breach of defensive walls
    or strategic maneuvers
air becomes less dense, light dims
quickly after the safe comfort of the
    cave's vestibule
          repelling deeper
              confronting the sump.

While suspended in the cold dark womb
    of disorientation,
I attempt to decipher the petroglyphs,
clinging to a long rope tied with a knot
    that strengthens under a load.
I've learned to tie a bowline with one hand.
    The rabbit comes out of the hole
          around the tree
            and back into the hole.

Bit Parts

He boxed up his memories,
all his secrets, and returned
to his rural hometown after
decades of fruitless auditions
for various roles,
          mostly bit parts.

On the road, he thought about
a Samurai sword exhibition
he saw in a show at a hospital
he visited on a trip to revisit
places where he had been
          stationed in Japan.

Once home, he began to clear
the land of debris and trash,
dead shrubs, and diseased trees.
He felt renewed. One evening,
he sat on the porch to marvel
          at his progress.

In fading light, he recalled
his mother taking him
and his younger sister to pick
wild blackberries by the creek,
long since diverted for some reason
          no one could remember.

The Edge of the World

Looking at the map,
you asked me to find
Patagonia.
I once knew a man from
Patagonia,
he wore a white shirt
every day of his life
until the day he died.
He wore a blue shirt
at church one day,
everyone he knew
became so disoriented
he rectified the anomaly
by midday.
He often spoke of his
Welsh ancestors who
sailed from Liverpool on
the *Mimosa* and settled
during midwinter in the
Chubut Valley.
His ancestors packed
all their dreams for a
better world and tearfully
said goodbye to their
homeland. They carried
with them their language,
music, art, and literature.
Like most immigrants,
they wanted to celebrate
their culture without
fear, without reprisal.

At afternoon tea he
reveled in storytelling.
As a child, he listened to
BBC World radio programs
in Patagonian Welsh.
When a language dies,
the culture dies, he was
fond of saying,

our ancestors knew this,
it's up to us to honor
their sacrifices.

If our language dies, we die.
It's a story playing out
worldwide. That's why they
came here and it's why
we continue to thrive here
at the edge of world.

Ode To Leonard

Watching anonymous passersby
while smoking cigarettes inside
these walls, kids playing outside
living the life or living the dream

They were there yesterday, I think
I misplaced that memory thing

Some other day I'll check the frig,
the light inside no longer works

I read once all life depends on the sun,
tiny people working with wheelbarrows
full of chlorophyll until they retire,
making the brightest star a white dwarf

Do kids out there know the truth
as they hop and scotch and tic tac toe?

I will keep a keen eye out for them,
waiting, watching through this crack

That's how the light gets in you said
Maybe that's true, maybe it isn't

Hangin' with Goya

El sueño de la razón produce monstruos
        —Francisco Goya

He paced deep inside the black box
        where he'd been held captive
for God only knows how long.
Silence inside light and shadow
        betrays the working class
of the mind, he was sure of it.

Saturn devoured his children here
        with a blood moon mocking,
circling birds of prey hovering over
        a diviner's oak collapsed,
an altar destroyed by sparks from
        the mouths of envious enemies.

It's a grand plan unfolding
        to produce impossible *monstruos*,
fantasy abandoned by lucidity.
I too find no *sueño de la razón* here,
        only pulses of spider lightning
flashing against a sky of black holes.

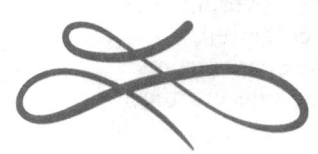

Albert and Vincent

V: What's it all about brother?

A: Space and time don't matter

V: That's what I've been thinking

A: The continuum is distorted

V: That's what I've been trying to say

A: The night sky reveals this grand truth

V: The night sky illuminates God's plan

A: I long to know God's thoughts one day

V: God gives us art so that we may see ourselves in it

A: The more I study science the more I believe in God

V: The more I study nature the more I believe in God

A: God, the most difficult question

Kenneth Johnson is a poet, visual artist, and educator living in Claremont, California. He received his MA.Ed from California State University at Pomona. After a career teaching art and art history courses, he now dedicates his time to creating art and writing poetry in both English and Spanish.

He can be reached at his website:
kennethjohnsonart.wixsite.com/kennethjohnsonart

www.ingramcontent.com/pod-product-compliance
Lightning Source LLC
Chambersburg PA
CBHW031240120626
46545CB00003B/1215